About Money

by Mary Reina

Consulting Editor: Gail Saunders-Smith, PhD

Consultant: Dr. Sharon M. Danes
Professor, Family Social Science Department
University of Minnesota

CAPSTONE PRESS
a capstone imprint

Pebble Books are published by Capstone Press,
1710 Roe Crest Drive, North Mankato, Minnesota 56003
www.capstonepub.com

Library of Congress Cataloging-in-Publication Data
Reina, Mary.
Learn about money / by Mary Reina.
pages cm. — (Pebble books. Money and you.)
Audience: K to Grade 3.
Includes bibliographical references and index.
Summary: "Introduces young readers to different types of money and how people
can use it to buy goods and services"— Provided by publisher.
ISBN 978-1-4914-2084-3 (library binding)
ISBN 978-1-4914-2302-8 (paperback)
ISBN 978-1-4914-2306-6 (eBook PDF)
1. Money—Juvenile literature. I. Title.
HG221.5.R45 2015
332.4—dc23   2014022150

Editorial Credits
Michelle Hasselius, editor; Kazuko Collins, designer;
Gina Kammer, media researcher; Kathy McColley, production specialist

Photo Credits
iStockphotos: mrundbaken, 6; Shutterstock: Arvind Balaraman, 16, Creativa Images,
18, Eldad Carin, 10, Luna Vandoorne, 4, Napatsan Puakpong, 14, Natali Glado, 12,
Ragnarock, 8, slavapolo, cover, Vinicius Tupinamba, 20
Design Elements: Shutterstock: elic (background), kavalenkava volha (coin)

Note to Parents and Teachers

The Money and You set supports national social studies standards related to production,
distribution, and consumption. This book describes and illustrates different types of money.
The images support early readers in understanding the text. The repetition of words and
phrases helps early readers learn new words. This book also introduces early readers to
subject-specific vocabulary words, which are defined in the Glossary section. Early readers
may need assistance to read some words and to use the Table of Contents, Glossary, Read
More, Internet Sites, and Index sections in the book.

Printed in the United States of America in Stevens Point, Wisconsin.
092014 008479WZS15

Table of Contents

A Helpful Tool

Money lets us buy and
sell goods and services.
The money we use today
was not used long ago.
Money has changed over time.

cowrie shells

People used objects they wanted or needed as money. Cowrie shells were used as money in China in 1200 B.C.

currency from different
countries around the world

8

Currency

Today we use paper bills and metal coins as money. Each country has its own money. It's called currency.

 penny = 1 cent

 nickel = 5 cents

 dime = 10 cents

 quarter = 25 cents

In the United States, we use dollars and cents as currency. Pennies, nickels, dimes, and quarters all equal a certain number of cents.

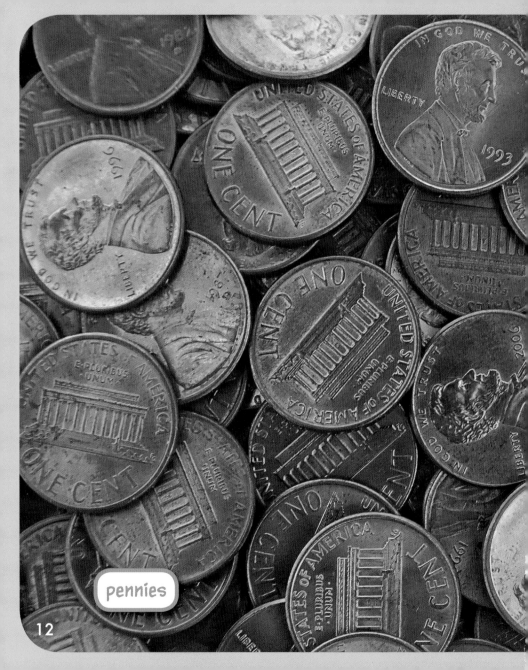
pennies

U.S. currency includes paper bills worth a certain number of dollars. One dollar is worth 100 pennies.

Japanese yen

Other countries use other currencies. People use yen in Japan. They use pesos in Mexico. People in Italy use euros.

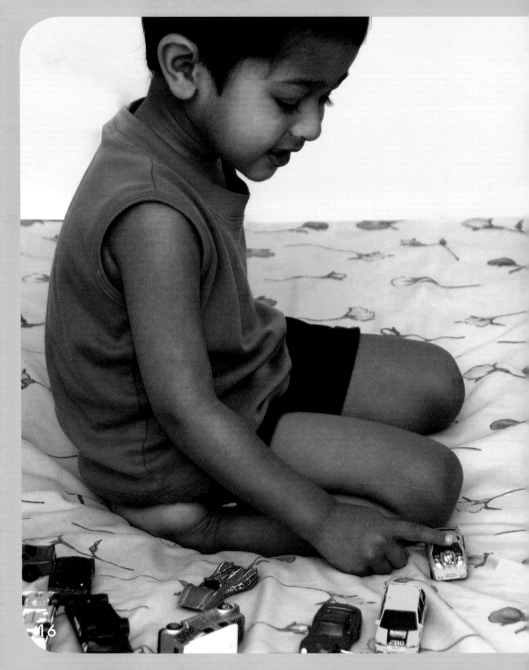

Other Kinds of Money

Rory sells Kim a toy car for $1 on credit. Credit is money borrowed to be paid later. Usually you pay extra money when you use credit.

Carrie's mom buys a book on the Internet. She pays online. The money is taken from her bank account electronically.

Money has changed over time. It may change again. Someday you may use a new kind of money.

Glossary

bank account—an account where a person keeps his or her money

bill—a piece of paper used as money

coin—a small piece of metal used as money

credit—money borrowed to buy something; people must pay credit back later

currency—the type of money a country uses

electronic—powered by electricity; electricity is a form of energy

goods—items that can be bought or sold

Internet—a system that connects computers all over the world; people buy items on the Internet

Read More

Larson, Jennifer S. *What Is Money Anyway?: Why Dollars and Coins Have Value.* Exploring Economics. Minneapolis: Lerner Publications Co., 2010.

Penn, M.W. *Counting Money!* Pebble Math. North Mankato, Minn.: Capstone Press, 2012.

Reid, Margarette S. *Lots and Lots of Coins.* New York: Dutton Children's Books, 2011.

Internet Sites

FactHound offers a safe, fun way to find Internet sites related to this book. All of the sites on FactHound have been researched by our staff.

Here's all you do:
Visit *www.facthound.com*
Type in this code: 9781491420843

Check out projects, games and lots more at
www.capstonekids.com

Critical Thinking Using the Common Core

1. Countries use different kinds of currency. What is currency? Name a type of currency we use in the United States. (Craft and Structure)

2. Turn to page 18. What do you think is happening in the picture? Use the text on page 19 to help you with your answer. (Integration of Knowledge and Ideas)

Index

Word Count: 188
Grade: 1
Early-Intervention Level: 20